by Elise Petrie

SCHOOL PUBLISHERS

Cover (background) ©Photolibrary.com; (main) ©Harcourt Index; 3–7 ©Photolibrary.com; 8–9 ©Getty Images; 10 ©Photolibrary.com; 11 ©Alamy; 12–13 ©Photolibrary.com; 14 (tl) ©Photolibrary.com; (tr) ©Photolibrary.com; (bl) ©Getty Images; (br) Photolibrary.com.

Printed in China

ISBN 10: 0-15-350419-6
ISBN 13: 978-0-15-350419-8

Ordering Options
ISBN 10: 0-15-350332-7 (Grade 2 Below-Level Collection)
ISBN 13: 978-0-15-350332-0 (Grade 2 Below-Level Collection)
ISBN 10: 0-15-357440-2 (package of 5)
ISBN 13: 978-0-15-357440-5 (package of 5)

4 5 6 7 8 9 10   0940   15 14 13 12 11 10 09

Many animal babies live in
the mountains.

Baby Bears

Baby brown bears are born in a den in winter. At first, they have no fur. Their mother's coat keeps them warm.

The baby bears stay inside until
spring. Then they go outside. They
learn from their mother where to
find food.

Baby Lynx

Lynx are part of the cat family.
Baby lynx are born in a den in
spring. Their mother cares for
them until the next winter.

Baby lynx have thick fur on their
paws. This helps them run fast
over deep snow. It is cold, but
sweat may come out of their paws!

Baby Snowshoe Hares

Baby snowshoe hares are born
in the forest. At first, they have
brown fur and ears. The ears are
about as long as your thumb.

Baby hares have large feet.
This helps them run fast over
the snow.

Baby Mountain Goats

A baby mountain goat is born in winter. Soon it can run with its mother. Its father is off in the mountains.

The mother and baby join other
mountain goat mothers and babies.
The babies play together.

Baby Porcupines

A baby porcupine is born in a den. Its quills are soft. Soon the quills become hard.

The baby porcupine learns from its mother which leaves are good to eat.

The mountains are home to many
kinds of baby animals.

Think Critically

1. What mountain babies are born in winter?

2. Why are the mothers of the babies important?

3. How is the information in this book organized?

4. Which mountain baby do you like the best? Why?

5. Is this a fiction or a nonfiction book about mountain babies? How can you tell?

 Science

Make a Fact File Choose one of the babies in the book and write all the facts you learned about that animal. Draw a picture of the animal.

School-Home Connection Ask a family member to tell you about when you were a baby. Tell that person some things you learned about mountain babies.

Word Count: 228